Just So Stories on Stage

A collection of plays based on Rudyard Kipling's Just So Stories

Julie Meighan

First published in 2017
by
JemBooks
Cork,
Ireland
www.dramastartbooks.com

ISBN: 978-0-9935506-4-5

Just So Stories on Stage

A collection of plays based on Rudyard Kipling's Just So Stories

Julie Meighan

JemBooks

Julie Meighan

About the Author

Julie runs an educational blog at http://dramastartbooks.com where she writes about all aspects of drama in education. She has written several books for teachers on the subject. Her books have been translated into several languages and to date have sold over 30,000 copies. Julie is currently a lecturer in Drama at Cork Institute of Technology, Cork, Ireland where she lectures on the Early Years Education and Social Care degree courses. She has delivered drama workshops and training to a wide variety of academic and professional organisations worldwide.

Rudyard Kipling (1856-1936)

Rudyard Kipling was born on December 30, 1865, in Bombay, India. He was educated in England but he returned to India in 1882. He was considered one of the greatest British writers of his generation. Kipling's experiences in India formed the basis of stories. His short stories were compiled into an anthology of 40 short stories called *Plain Tales from the Hills*. This book became very popular in England. He moved to Vermont where he wrote *The Jungle Book* (1894), *The Naulahka: A Story of the West and East (1892)* and *The Second Jungle Book* (1895). By the age of 32, Kipling was the highest paid writer in the world. He received the Nobel Prize for Literature in 1907.

Julie Meighan

Contents

nilo: camei Da D! man uncle Blake!
Aora! Horse mom story 1 story 2
tob 'ox aunt tan! story3
mac! Djin Link; Dog

How the Camel Got His Hump

Characters: Three storytellers, Camel, Man, Ox, Horse, Dog, Djinn.

Storyteller 1: In the beginning when the world was new.

Storyteller 2: All the animals were working hard to make the world a better place.

Storyteller 3: Except for the camel who was very lazy. The camel lived in the middle of the Howling desert.

Camel: Look at all those animals running around working. I'm going to sit here relax and much on some sticks, stones and tamarisks. Humph.

Storyteller 1: On Monday, the horse came trotting by.

Horse: Neigh, neigh, Camel, come and trot like the rest of us.

Camel: Humph.

Horse: Is that all you must say? Humph

Camel: *(nods his head)* Humph, just humph.

(Horse trots off and meets the man.)

Horse: That camel is SO lazy.

Storyteller 2: After a while dog came by. He had a stick in his mouth.

Dog: woof, wolf, Camel, come and fetch and carry like the rest of us.

Camel: Humph.

Dog: Is that all you have to say? Humph

Camel: *(nods his head)* Humph, just humph.

(Dog bounds off and meets the man.)

Dog: That camel is SO lazy.

Storyteller 2: Soon an ox passed by. He had a yoke on his neck.

Ox: woof, wolf, Camel, come and plough and carry like the rest of us.

Camel: Humph.

Ox: Is that all you have to say? Humph

Camel: *(nods his head)* Humph, just humph.

(Ox slowly moves off and meets the man.)

Ox: That camel is SO lazy.

1

Julie Meighan

Storyteller 3: At the end of the day. The man called the horse, the dog and the ox together and said...

DaD **Man:** I'm very sorry for you (with the world so new-and-all); but that Humph-thing in the Desert doesn't seem to be able to do any work, so I am going to leave him alone, but I'm afraid you must work twice as hard to make up for it.

Horse: Well that's not very fair, is it?

Man: Life isn't fair sometimes.

Dog: We worked hard all day.

Ox: I'm very angry with that humph thing in the dessert.

Camel: Ha, ha. Why would I work? When I can sit here and be scrumptiously idle.

mUm **Storyteller 1:** Presently along came the djinn of all dessert. *(He comes rolling in.)*

Horse: Djinn of All Deserts, sit right for anyone to be idle, with the world so new-and-all?'

Djinn: Of course not. Why do you ask?

Horse: There is a thing in the middle of your Howling Desert with a long neck and long legs, and he hasn't done a stroke of work since Monday morning. He won't trot.'

Dog: He says "Humph! 'and he won't fetch and carry.

max **Djinn:** Does he say anything else?

Ox: Only "Humph!"; and he won't plough,

Djinn: I'll humph him if you will kindly wait a minute.

Djinn: What's all this I hear about you being bone idle?

Camel: Humph, Just humph.

Djinn: All the animals have had to work twice as hard since you won't pull your weight.

Camel: Humph, just humph.

Djinn: I really wouldn't say Humph again if I were you,

Camel: Humph, just humph.

Storyteller 3: The Djinn used some magic and suddenly a hump grew on the camel's back. And the Camel said 'Humph!' again; but no sooner had he said it than he saw his back, that he was so proud of, puffing up and puffing up into a great big lolloping humph.

Camel: Djinn, what have you done?

Djinn: Now you can work for three days because that hump on your back will keep your food and drink in it for three days.

2

Storyteller 1: And the Camel humphed himself, humph and all, and went away to join the other three.
Storyteller 2: And from that day to this the Camel always wears a humph (we call it 'hump' now, not to hurt his feelings);
Storyteller 3: But he has never yet caught up with the three days that he missed at the beginning of the world, and he has never yet learned how to behave.

THE Camel's hump is an ugly lump
Which well you may see at the Zoo;
But uglier yet is the hump we get
From having too little to do.

Kiddies and grown-ups too-of-oo,
If we haven't enough to do-oo-oo,
We get the hump—
Cameelious hump—
The hump that is black and blue!

We climb out of bed with a frouzly head
And a snarly-yarly voice.
We shiver and scowl and we grunt and we growl
At our bath and our boots and our toys;

And there ought to be a corner for me
(And I know there is one for you)
When we get the hump—
Cameelious hump—
The hump that is black and blue!

The cure for this ill is not to sit still,
Or frowst with a book by the fire;
But to take a large hoe and a shovel also,
And dig till you gently perspire;

And then you will find that the sun and the wind,
And the Djinn of the Garden too,
Have lifted the hump—

3

Julie Meighan

The horrible hump—
The hump that is black and blue!

I get it as well as you-oo-oo—
If I haven't enough to do-oo-oo—
We all get hump—
Cameelious hump—
Kiddies and grown-ups too!

How the Elephant Got His Trunk

Characters: Three narrators, Elephant Child, Ostrich, Giraffe, Hippo, Python, Crocodile, Koloko Bird, Fly, Mother Elephant, Father Elephant

Narrator 1: Once upon a time, a long, long, time ago on the plains of Africa...

Narrator 2: ...there lived elephants who did not have any trunks.

Narrator 3: Instead, they had a little snout just like pigs have today. They couldn't drink through their snout.

Narrator 1: Nor could they pick up anything.

Narrator 2: There lived one elephant child who was very curious.

Narrator 3: He was always asking questions. He asked the Ostrich:

Elephant child: Ostrich, why do you bury your head?

Ostrich: I bury my head in the sand because I'm shy and don't like talking to people. Now, go away.

Elephant Child: Giraffe, why is your neck so long?

Giraffe: Because I'm very nosy and I like to see what his going on in the jungle.

Elephant Child: Hippo, why are your eyes so red?

Hippo: Because I swim in dirty water all day and it hurts my eyes.

Narrator 1: He asked questions about everything that he saw, smelt, felt, touched or tasted.

Narrator 2: One morning he had a new question that he had never asked before.

Elephant Child: I wonder what a crocodile has for dinner.

(All the animals tell him to be quiet and to stop asking such silly questions.)

Elephant Child: Fine. If you won't tell me, I'll ask the Koloko Bird. Koloko Bird, what does a crocodile have for dinner?

Koloko Bird: I don't know, but there is one way to find out.

Elephant Child: How?

Koloko Bird: Ask him.

Narrator 3: The next morning, Elephant Child set off to find out what crocodiles ate for dinner.

Elephant Child: Goodbye, everyone. I am going to the great, grey, green, greasy river to find out what crocodiles have for dinner.

Narrator 1: He came across a python.

Elephant Child: Excuse me, sir, but have you seen such a thing as a crocodile in these parts?

Python: Mmm, have I seen a crocodile? Let me see. *(He thinks for a few seconds.)* Why yes, if you keep going straight, you will arrive at the great, grey, green, greasy river.

Elephant Child: Thank you, Python. *(He arrives at the river.)* Excuse me. Have you seen a crocodile?

Crocodile: Why, I am a crocodile. Look, I can cry crocodile tears. *(He begins to cry.)* How can I help you?

Elephant Child: Well, I have come all this way to ask you what you have for dinner.

Crocodile: Come closer and I will tell you. *(Elephant Child moves closer.)* Closer, closer. *(He grabs Elephant Child by his nose.)* I think I will have an elephant's child for my dinner today.

Elephant Child: Let go of me. Help me, Python!

Narrator 1: Python pulled the elephant from behind.

Python: Koloko Bird, please help us. The Crocodile is trying to eat Elephant Child for his dinner.

Narrator 2: Python and Koloko Bird pulled the elephant from behind.

Koloko bird: Hippo, please help us. Crocodile is trying to eat Elephant Child for his dinner.

Narrator 3: Python, Koloko Bird and Hippo pulled the elephant from behind.

Hippo: Giraffe, please help us. Crocodile is trying to eat Elephant Child for his dinner.

Narrator 1: Python, Koloko Bird, Hippo and Giraffe pulled the elephant from behind.

Giraffe: Ostrich, please help us. Crocodile is trying to eat Elephant Child for his dinner.

Narrator 2: They all pulled the elephant from behind very hard and eventually Crocodile let go. *(They all fall on the ground and the crocodile swims off.)*

Elephant Child: Oh dear, look at my nose. It is all out of shape and it is way too long.

(A fly buzzes by and the elephant swats it with his trunk.)

Python: You couldn't have done that with your old nose.

Narrator 3: The elephant was hungry and he picked up some grass with his new nose.

Koloko Bird: You couldn't have done that with your old nose.

Narrator 3: Elephant Child was very hot and he sucked up water with his new nose and sprayed himself.

Hippo: You couldn't have done that with your old nose.

Narrator 1: Elephant Child went home to show off his new nose.

Mother Elephant: What did you do to your nose?

Elephant Child: I got a new nose from the crocodile on the banks of the great, grey, green, greasy river.

Narrator 2: He showed them all the new things he could do with his nose.

Father Elephant: How very useful. I want one of those.

Narrator 3: All the elephants saw how useful it was and one by one they went to the great, grey, green, greasy river to get new noses from the crocodile. The crocodile did a roaring trade until all the elephants in the jungle had long trunks like Elephant Child.

Crocodile: Roll up! Roll up! Get your new elephant noses here.

Julie Meighan

How the Whale got his Throat

Characters: Three storytellers, Whale, Stute fish, Marnier, the rest of the class can be diverse types of fish.

Storyteller 1: Once upon a time, long, long time ago, deep, deep in the ocean.

Storyteller 2: There lived a whale. He loved to eat fish.

Storyteller 3: He ate the starfish and the garfish, and the crab and the dab, and the plaice and the dace, and the skate and his mate, and the mackerel and the pickerel, and the truly twirly-whirly eel.
(Children can pretend to be the different fish. They move around to music. Eventually the whale eats them all.)

Stute Fish: The whale has eaten all the fish in the sea. I'm next unless I'm very, very clever.

Whale: I'm hungry.

Stute fish: I'm small enough to swim behind his ear so he won't see me.

Whale: I'm so hungry and I've eaten all the fish

Stute Fish: Oh, noble and generous whale you ever tasted man?

Whale: What was that? *(Looks shocked)* Man, no I've never tasted man. What is it like?

Stute Fish: Nice and bubbly.

Whale: Where would I find this man to eat?

Stute Fish: If you swim to latitude Fifty North, longitude Forty West (that is magic), you will find, sitting *on* a raft, *in* the middle of the sea, with nothing on but a pair of blue canvas breeches, a pair of suspenders (you must *not* forget the suspenders, Best Beloved), and a jack-knife, one ship-wrecked Mariner, who, it is only fair to tell you, is a man of infinite-resource-and-sagacity.'

Storyteller 1: So, the Whale swam and swam to latitude Fifty North, longitude Forty West, as fast as he could swim, and *on* a raft, *in* the middle of the sea, *with* nothing to wear except a pair of blue canvas breeches, a pair of suspenders (you must particularly remember the suspenders, Best Beloved), *and* a jack-knife, he found one single, solitary shipwrecked Mariner, trailing his toes in the water. (He had his mummy's leave to paddle, or else he would never have done it, because he was a man of infinite-resource-and-sagacity.)

Whale: There he is I found him.

Storyteller 2: So, the whale opens his mouth as far as he could and swallowed the mariner whole.

But as soon as the Mariner, who was a man of infinite-resource-and-sagacity, found himself truly inside the Whale's warm, dark, inside cup-board.

Storyteller 3: He stumped and he jumped and he thumped and he bumped, and he pranced and he danced, and he banged and he clanged, and he hit and he bit, and he leaped and he creeped, and he prowled and he howled, and he hopped and he dropped, and he cried and he sighed, and he crawled and he bawled, and he stepped and he lepped, and he danced hornpipes where he shouldn't, and the Whale felt most unhappy indeed. (*Have* you forgotten the suspenders?)

Whale: This man is very nubbly, and besides he is making me hiccough. What shall I do?'

Stute Fish: Tell him to come out.

Whale: Come out and behave yourself. I've got the hiccoughs.'

Marnier: No unless you take me to my natal-shore and the white-cliffs-of-Albion, and I'll think about it.

Storyteller 1: And he began to dance more than ever.

Stute Fish: You had better take him home. I ought to have warned you that he is a man of infinite-resource-and-sagacity.'

Storyteller 2: So, the Whale swam and swam and swam, with both flippers and his tail, as hard as he could for the hiccoughs; and at last he saw the Mariner's natal-shore and the white-cliffs-of-Albion, and he rushed half-way up the beach, and opened his mouth wide and wide and wide, and said...

Whale: Change here for Winchester, Ashkelon, Nashua, Keene, and stations on the *Fitch*burg Road;

Storyteller 3: And just as he said 'Fitch' the Mariner walked out of his mouth. But while the Whale had been swimming, the Mariner, who was indeed a person of infinite-resource-and-sagacity, had taken his jack-knife and cut up the raft into a little square grating all running criss-cross, and he had tied it firm with his suspenders (*now*, you know why you were not to forget the suspenders!), and he dragged that grating good and tight into the Whale's throat, and there it stuck!

Marnier: By the means of a grating, I've stopped your ating.

Storyteller 1: From that day on, the grating in his throat, which he could neither cough up nor swallow down, prevented him eating anything except very, very small fish;

Storyteller 2: And that is the reason why whales nowadays never eat men or boys or little girls.

Storyteller 3: The small 'Stute Fish went and hid himself in the mud under the Door-sills of the Equator. He was afraid that the Whale might be angry with him.

When the cabin port-holes are dark and green
Because of the seas outside;
When the ship goes *wop* (with a wiggle between)
And the steward falls into the soup-tureen,
And the trunks begin to slide;
When Nursey lies on the floor in a heap,
And Mummy tells you to let her sleep,
And you aren't waked or washed or dressed,
Why, then you will know (if you haven't guessed)
You're 'Fifty North and Forty West!'

How the Rhinoceros got his Skin

Characters: Two narrators; Hippopotamus; Camel; Giraffe; Horned Viper; two gazelles; ostriches (as many as you need); two striped hyenas; Rhinoceros; Parsee Man.

(Stage Directions: Curtains open on all the animals in the jungle. They dance to animal-style music.)

Narrator 1: Long ago on an island on the shores of the Red Sea, there lived a Parsee Man and lots of animals. They would work together to collect food to last throughout the summer's drought.
(All the animals milling around the stage, they all mime doing work such as fetching and carrying.)
Narrator 2: The only animal that didn't pull its weight was a very, very, very lazy rhinoceros. The rhinoceros would sit around doing nothing, his knobby legs protruding from under his fat stomach.
(Rhino is sitting on the left side of stage, resting.)
Narrator 1: The Camel, who was considered the wisest animal in all of Egypt, would sometimes scold the Rhino. *(Camel and Horned Viper walk toward Rhino. All the other animals are busy working.)*
Camel: Rhino, don't you think you should help everyone else? We all must collect food and water so we do not starve in the sweltering summer.
Horned Viper: Yes, you know how hot it gets. Everything dies. We must make sure we have enough food to survive.
Rhino: Oh, go away, I'm busy relaxing here under the warm shade.
(Rhino starts laughing and shoos them away.)
Giraffe: *(Puts his arm around Camel.)* Do not take any notice of him, Camel. He is not a nice animal. Rhino is foolish.
Horned Viper: Come on, Camel and Giraffe, we don't need him. We can ask the other animals to help us.
(Parsee Man enters the stage.)
Parsee Man: Why do you look so glum, Camel?
Hippopotamus: Hello, Parsee Man. Camel asked Rhino to help us collect food for the winter, but he just wants to relax under the shady tree.

Horned Viper: While we do all the work!

Parsee Man: Don't take any notice of him. I will help you. I will make you my special cake. This will give you energy to collect food for the summer.

Camel: What a splendid idea. Giraffe, call the ostriches. Horned Viper, get the gazelles and I will get striped hyenas.

Hippopotamus: We can all collect the food and have a big party afterwards with the cake the Parsee Man makes.

Parsee Man: I will make the most superior cake I've ever made.

(The Parsee Man gets all the ingredients. He holds them up one by one and then he mimes mixing them in a bowl.)

Parsee Man: Now, let me see. What do I need? Some flour, water, currants, plums, sugar, and a few other things.

Striped Hyena 1: Look at that lazy rhino. He has done nothing all day except lie there under the shady tree.

Gazelle 1: Ignore him. He has no Parsee Manners, no Parsee Manners at all.

Ostriches: The rhino will never have manners even if he lives to be a hundred.

Striped Hyena 2: Let's get back to work. We have the Parsee Man's cake to look forward to later.

Rhino: All those animals are ridiculous. I'm enjoying the sunshine. *(He looks at his reflection in the water and admires himself.)* I'm so handsome. My skin is a perfect fit. None of the other animals' skin fits so well.

Narrator 1: The rhino fell back to sleep while all the other animal worked hard.

Narrator 2: The Parsee spent five weeks making the most splendid cake ever.

Parsee Man: Animals, come and I'll give you some cakes but remember
Them that take cakes
Which the Parsee-man bakes
Make dreadful mistakes.

(Parsee gives everyone a piece of cake. All the animals eat them and enjoy the party. Music can be played).

Rhino: What's going on over there? *(He sneaks over and sees all the animals eating the cake.)*

Camel: Thank you, Parsee Man, that is the most splendid cake I've ever eaten.

Horned Viper: It was worth working for five weeks just to eat one crumb of this cake.

Rhino: I want some cake. I will grab some when no one is looking.

(All the animals are dancing and enjoying themselves. Music is playing. The rhino slowly sneaks up and grabs the rest of the cake.)

Striped Hyenas: The cake is gone?

Gazelle 2: Look, I can see the rhino running off with it in the distance.

Parsee: Them that take cakes

Which the Parsee-man bakes

Make dreadful mistakes.

I've got a plan.

(He whispers to all the other animals and they laugh.)

Rhino: Yummy, that was the most superior cake I've ever eaten. I'm full and warm. I think I'll take a dip in the Red Sea.

Narrator: The rhino unzipped his skin and left by the side of the Red Sea.

(Parsee Man sneaks up to the skin. Presently, the Parsee man came by and found the skin. He smiled a smile that ran all the way round his face two times. Then he danced three times round the skin and rubbed his hands.)

Parsee Man: I've made the rest of the cake into crumbs. I'm going to put them into his skin. He is so proud of his smooth skin, I'm sure he won't be pleased when it turns all wrinkly. I'll throw extra currants in for good measure.

Narrator: Then he climbed to the top of his palm-tree and waited for the Rhinoceros to come out of the water and put it on.

Rhino: That was a very pleasant swim. Time to put on my skin; it's getting a bit chilly.

(He puts on the skin and buttons it up.)

Rhino: What happened to my smooth skin. It's all wrinkly now and so very itchy.

(He starts hoping up and down trying to scratch his back.)

Narrator: So, he went home, very angry indeed and horribly scratchy; and from that day to this every rhinoceros has great folds in his skin and a very bad temper, all because the cake-crumbs inside.

Parsee Man: And that my dear friends is how rhino got his skin.
(*Music starts playing and everyone starts dancing. The rhino is in a corner crying.*)

This Uninhabited Island
Is off Cape Gardafui.
By the Beaches of Socotra
And the Pink Arabian Sea:
But it's hot too hot from Suez
For the likes of you and me
Ever to go
In a P. and O.
And call on the Cake-Parsee!

How the Leopard Got His Spots

Characters: Four narrators, the leopard, the giraffe, the hunter, the zebra, the eland, the wildebeest and Baviaan, the wise dog-headed baboon.

Narrator 1: Long, long ago. There lived a leopard who lived on the High Veldt.
Narrator 2: The High Veldt had lots of sand, sandy coloured rock and sandy yellowish grass.
Narrator 3: The giraffe, the zebra, the eland and the hartebeest also lived in the sandy coloured High Veldt.
Narrator 4: All the animals were a sandy yellowish brownish colour but the sandy yellowish brownish of them all was the leopard.
Narrator 1: The leopard was the same colour as the High Veldt to the letter.
Narrator 2: The other animals did not like this fact, as they could never see the leopard when he was hunting.
(The giraffe and zebra walk along and the leopard jumps up and scares them. He runs after them. Then, the eland and hartebeest walk by and the leopard jumps up and scares them. He chases the eland and the hartebeest.)
(Along comes a hunter. The hunter is the same colour as the leopard.)
Hunter: Leopard, you are just as sandy coloured and yellowish as me.
(They compare their skin colour.)
Leopard: We are the same colour as the High Veldt.
Hunter: I have an idea. Let's go hunting together. I will hunt with my bow and arrow.
Leopard: And I will hunt with my teeth and claws.
(They go hunting. The other animals run left and right across the stage several times. The hunter is on the right side of the stage and the leopard is on the left side. Eventually, the chased animals are out of breath and they move to the centre of stage.)
Giraffe: What are we going to do?
Zebra: We can't roam peacefully on the High Veldt anymore because the hunter and the leopard are too difficult to spot.
Wildebeest: They are the same colour as the high veldt.

15

Eland: I think it may be a clever idea if we moved away.

Giraffe: Where would we go?

Zebra: I know a place; it is a great forest full of trees, bushes and striped, speckle, patchy, blotchy shadows.

Eland: What a clever idea. They will never find us there.

Wildebeest: We will be able to live peacefully.

All animals: Let's go!

Narrator 3: All the animals moved away from the High Veldt.

Narrator 4: They scuttled for days and days until they came to the great forest.

Narrator 1: One day the zebra noticed that the giraffe's skin colour had changed.

Zebra: Giraffe, look how blotchy your skin has become.

Giraffe: Do you like it? My skin has become blotchy because I'm standing in out and of the shade all day.

Zebra: What do you think of my black and white stripes?

Eland and Wildebeest: Zebra, you look very nice. We have become darker with little wavy lines on our back.

Giraffe: You look like the tree trunks.

Zebra: The leopard and the hunter would never find us here.

Narrator 2: Meanwhile on the High Veldt, the leopard and the hunter were getting very hungry.

Hunter: (*Looking around.*) Where have all the animals gone?

Narrator 3: They came across Baviaan, the barking dog-headed baboon.

Leopard: Let's ask Baviaan. He is the wisest animal in Africa.

Hunter: Where have all the animals gone?

Baviaan: The game has gone to the great big forest. My advice to you leopard is to change spots as soon as possible, and my advice to you hunter is just change.

Narrator 4: The hunter and the leopard were confused by the advice but they took off towards the forest.

Narrator 1: They travelled for days. They were about to give up when they saw the great big forest, full of tree trunks

Leopard: What is this place? It is so very dark but full of little pieces of light. (*They both looked around the forest in amazement.*)

Hunter: This just gets curiouser and curiouser. I can smell a giraffe and I can hear a giraffe but I can't see a giraffe.

Leopard: I can smell and zebra and I can hear a zebra but I can't see one.

(The giraffe and the zebra are moving around the stage quietly; when the leopard or the hunter looks at them, they freeze.)

Narrator 2: The hunter and the leopard waited until dark and pretended to sleep.

Narrator 3: The leopard heard something breathing heavily and he jumped on the noise.

(The leopard jumps on the zebra and wrestles him to the ground. The zebra struggles but then stops.)

Leopard: Be quite and stop struggling. I'm going to sit on your head until the morning and then I will see who you really are.

Narrator 4: From a distance, there was another crashing noise. The hunter had caught something else.

(Hunter captures the giraffe and wrestles him to the floor.)

Hunter: I caught something. It smells like a giraffe and feels like a giraffe but it doesn't have any form.

Leopard: Sit on its head until the morning and you will see its true form in the light.

Narrator 1: Morning came, eventually.

Leopard: What have you got at the end of the table, Brother?

(Hunter looks at the giraffe strangely and scratches his head.)

Hunter: It is most peculiar. It looks like a giraffe and smells like a giraffe but it is covered all over with brown blotches. What have you captured, Brother?

(Leopard looks at the zebra strangely and scratches his head.)

Leopard: Well, it looks like a zebra and smells like a zebra but it has these black and whites stripes all over its body. *(Looks at the zebra.)* Zebra, what have you being doing? Don't you know that if you were on the High Veldt, I would be able to see you for miles?

Zebra: We are not in the High Veldt now, Leopard.

Leopard: How did this happen?

Zebra: If you let us get up, we can show you.

Narrator 2: They let the giraffe and the zebra go. The zebra moved towards some bushes where the sunlight fell all in stripes and he disappeared. The giraffe moved towards some tall trees where he suddenly vanished.

Zebra and Giraffe: *(Laughing.)* Where's you breakfast, now?

Leopard: Where did they go?

17

Hunter: That is a clever trick. (*He looks at the leopard.*) Leopard, you could learn a lesson from them. You show up like a bar of soap in a coal bucket.

Leopard: Ha, ha. You can't talk. You show up in this forest like a mustard plaster on a sack of coals.

Hunter: Well, laughing at how silly we look won't catch breakfast. Remember what Baviaan told me. He said, I should change but I've nothing to change but my skin. I'm going to change my skin to blackish brown so I can hide behind trees and in hollows.

Narrator 3: The hunter changed his skin colour there and then.

Leopard: What about me?

Hunter: Take Baviaan's advice. He told you to go into spots. I'll dip my fingers in this paint and put spots all over your body. (*Hunter puts the tips of his fingers all over the leopard.*)

Leopard: You must make them small. I don't want to look like giraffe.

Hunter: You look beautiful. Now, you can lie on rocks and look like a piece of stone or lie on a tree and look like sunshine shifting through the leaves.

Leopard: Let's go find some breakfast.

Narrator 4: And off they went into the deep forest and lived happily ever after, and they were never hungry again.

The Cat That Walked by Himself

Characters: Two Narrators, Dog, Horse, Sheep, Pig, Man, Woman, Bat, Mouse and Baby.

Narrator 1: This is the story of "The Cat That Walked by Himself" and it happened just so. Long, long ago when the world was new, all the tame animals were wild.

Dog: I'm wild.

Horse: I'm wilder.

Cow: I'm as wild as can be.

Narrator 2: But the animal that was the wildest of all was…

Cat: I'm the wildest animal in the woods. I'm so wild that I'm the cat that walks by himself in the Wet Wild Woods. All places are alike to me.

Man: I was wild too, like the animals.

Woman: Until he met me and I tamed him. I choose a nice warm cave and lit a cosy fire.

Man: Now we live a very tame life.

(Man attempts to enter the cave.)

Woman: Wipe your feet on the mat, dear.

Man: Oh, sorry. I like being tame. I get to eat nice food and sleep by a cosy fire every night.

Narrator 1: One night, while the man was sleeping, the woman found a shoulder bone of mutton.

Woman: Look at this bone. It has wonderful markings. I think I'll make something out of it.

Narrator 1: The woman worked all night carving the bone.

Woman: There, that's finished. I've made the first singing magic in the entire world.

(Magic starts playing music.)

Horse: What's that wonderful sound?

Dog: It's coming from the cave. *(Dog starts sniffing.)* I'll go to the cave and find out what is making that beautiful sound. Cat, come with me.

Cat: No, I won't come with you. I'm the cat that walks by himself.

Dog: Fine, suit yourself. I'm off to the cave.

Cat: It's true, I'm the cat that walks by himself, but I must say, I'm a little curious. I wonder if I snuck up to the cave and had a look around if anyone would see.

Dog: What's that beautiful sound?

Woman: It's the first singing magic.

Dog: Something smells good in here.

(Woman picks up a large mutton bone and throws it at the dog.)

Dog: That's delicious. May I have some more?

Woman: You want some more? Well, if you help the man during the day and if you guard our cave at night, you can have all the bones you want.

Dog: Deal.

(Woman shakes Dog's paw with her hand.)

Cat: The dog is selling his wildness for a bone. That woman is very wise and that is a foolish dog.

(Cat storms off back into the woods.)

Narrator 2: The next night, while the man slept soundly in the cave, the woman made herself busy.

Woman: I think I'll make a second singing magic.

Narrator 1: She worked on the singing magic all evening. When it was finished, it made the most beautiful sound.

Horse: I wonder why the dog hasn't returned. I'll go to the cave and find out. Cat, please come with me.

Cat: No, I won't go to the cave with you. I am the cat that walks by himself.

Narrator 2: However, curiosity got the cat, so he followed the horse to the cave. The cat listened very carefully outside the cave.

Horse: Neigh, neigh where is the dog?

Woman: Horse, you are fooling no one. You didn't come here because you're looking for the dog. You came here because you're hungry. If you take this halter, you can eat delicious grass three times a day.

Cat: That woman is very clever but not as clever as I am.

Horse: Neigh, neigh. Mistress, Master, I will be your loyal servant if you promise me grass three times a day.

(Woman gives the halter to the horse and he wears it proudly.)

Cat: What a foolish horse. *(Cat walks off but meets the cow.)* Where are you going, Cow?

Cow: I'm going up to the cave. I'm going to give the woman my milk if she lets me graze on her grass.

Narrator 1: The cat wasn't pleased with the dog, the horse and the cow but the next night he decided to go to the cave.

Woman: Oh, look what the cat dragged in – A CAT.

Cat: I came to see my friend, the cow.

Woman: You didn't. You want some of this warm white milk, but we have no use for you in this cave.

Cat: Aren't you going to invite me into your warm cave?

Woman: You should have come the first night the dog asked you to come.

Cat: Has that foolish dog been telling tales about me?

Woman: You are the cat that walks by himself, so walk by yourself.

Cat: Why are you so cruel? You are a very wise and beautiful woman.

Woman: Well, I know I'm wise, but no one has called me beautiful, so if I ever say one word in your praise, you can come into the cave. If I say two words in your praise, you may sit by the fire.

Cat: And three words?

Woman: That, my dear, shall never happen but if I do, you may drink some milk.

Narrator 2: The cat left the cave and walked by himself. Months passed. One night the cat met the upside-down bat.

Cat: Good evening, Bat. Any news?

Bat: Funny you should ask. I have some news. There's a baby in the cave. He is new and pink and fat and small. The woman loves the baby more than the man, the dog, the horse, the cow or the dog.

Cat: Babies are fond of cats.

Bat: Yes, babies like cats because cats are soft and tickly.

Cat: My time has come.

Narrator 1: The cat crept up to the cave. The woman was cooking and the baby was crying. The cat went over to the baby and tickled him.

Cat: Hello, Baby. I'll tickle you with my paddy paw.

Narrator 2: The baby stopped crying and started smiling and then laughing.

Bat: Oh, Mistress, a wild thing is playing with your baby.

Woman: Well, that wild thing has managed to stop him from crying. The wild thing is a blessing that has done me a very big favour. The baby hasn't stopped crying all day and all night.

Cat: It is I, the cat that walks by himself. You've given me one word of praise.

Woman: I'm true to my word. You can now sit in the warm, cozy cave.

Cat: For always and always and always.

Narrator 2: The cat sat by the fire and began singing a lullaby to the baby.

Cat: Rock-a-bye baby on the tree top, when the wind blows the baby will rock

(Baby yawns and falls asleep.)

Woman: Well done, Cat, you are so clever.

Cat: You have praised me twice, so now I can sit by the fire. I am the cat that walks by himself and all places are alike to me

Woman: Damn. I must make sure I don't praise him a third time.

Narrator 1: Suddenly, a mouse ran across the floor.

Woman: Shrieeeeeeeeeeeeeeeeek! (She jumps on a table.) Cat, do something. Get rid of that mouse.

(Cat jumps on the mouse and chases it out of the cave.)

Woman: Thank you, Cat. I'm ever so grateful.

Cat: You have praised me a third time. I can drink the warm milk. I'm the cat that walks by himself and all places are alike to me.

(Enter the man and the dog.)

Man: What is he doing here?

Woman: He was kind to the baby and got rid of the mouse.

Man: That is so. Now, Cat, make a bargain with me. If you don't catch mice whilst in the cave, I shall throw these five things at you whenever we meet. (The man takes off his boots, picks up his stone axe, and points to a hatchet and a piece of wood.)

Cat: I'll catch mice, but I'll never be your servant. I am the cat who walks by himself and all places are alike to me.

Man: You are an obstinate cat. I shall still throw three of these five things at you whenever we meet. *(He throws his boots and the stone axe at the cat.)*

Dog: Wait a minute. You haven't made a bargain with me. If you aren't kind to the baby, I shall hunt till I catch you, and when I catch you I'll bite you.

Cat: I'll be kind to babies if they don't pull my tail. I'm still the cat that walks by himself and all places are alike to me.

Dog: You are an obstinate cat. I will chase you up a tree whenever we meet.

Narrator 1: Ever since then, three men out of five will chase a cat from the house and all dogs will chase a cat up a tree.

Narrator 2: However, the cat keeps his side of the bargain. He chases mice and is kind to babies when he is in the cave so long as they don't pull his tail.

Cat: But I'm still the cat that walks by himself and all places are alike to me.

Some day before I'm old!
Pussy can sit by the fire and sing,
Pussy can climb a tree,
Or play with a silly old cork and string
To 'muse herself, not me.
But I like *Binkie* my dog, because
He knows how to behave;
So, *Binkie's* the same as the First Friend was
And I am the Man in the Cave.

Pussy will play man-Friday till
It's time to wet her paw
And make her walk on the window-sill
 (For the footprint Crusoe saw);
Then she Ruffles her tail and mews,
And scratches and won't attend.
But *Binkie* will play whatever I choose,
And he is my true First Friend.

Pussy will rub my knees with her head
Pretending she loves me hard;
But the very minute I go to my bed
Pussy runs out in the yard,
And there she stays till the morning-light;

23

Julie Meighan

So I know it is only pretend;
But *Binkie*, he snores at my feet all night,
And he is my Firstest Friend!

The Crab that Played with the Sea

Characters: Three Narrators, Eldest Magician, Man, Girl Daughter, Pau Amma (crab), Elephants, Beavers, Cows, Turtles, Fisher of the Moon, Rat of the Moon. (There can be as many elephants, beavers, cows and turtles as you wish.)

Narrator 1: This is the story of the crab that played with the sea, and it happened just so. Long, long ago when the world was new and all, the Eldest Magician was getting things ready.
Narrator 2: First he got the Earth ready.
Narrator 3: Then he got the sea ready. Then he told all the animals that they could come out and play.
Eldest Magician: Animals, come out, come out, wherever you are. Come and play. (*All the animals come out slowly. They seem unsure what to do.*)
Animals: Eldest Magician, what shall we play?
Eldest Magician: I will show you.
Narrator 1: He took the elephants—all-the-elephants-there-were—and said:
Eldest Magician: Play at being an elephant. (*All the elephants start digging with their tusks and stomping their feet.*)
Narrator 2: He took the beavers—all-the-beavers-there-were—and said:
Eldest Magician: Play at being a beaver. (*All the beavers start cutting down trees.*)
Narrator 3: He took the cows—all-the-cows-there-were—and said:
Eldest Magician: Play at being a cow. (*All the cows start grazing in the fields.*)
Narrator 1: He took the turtles— all-the-turtles-there-were—and said:
Eldest Magician: Play at being a turtle. (*All the turtles dig deep in the sand with their flippers.*)
Narrator 2: One by one, he took all the beasts and birds and fishes and told them what to play.
Narrator 3: However, towards evening, when people and things grow restless and tired, the Man arrived with his little Girl Daughter.

Man: What is this play, Eldest Magician?

Eldest Magician: Ho, Son of Adam, this is the play of the animals, but you are too wise for this play.

Man: Yes, I am too wise for this play, but see that you make all the animals obedient to me.

Narrator 3: Now, while the two were talking, Pau Amma the crab, who was next in the game, scuttled off sideways and stepped into the sea, saying to himself:

Pau Amma: I will play my play alone in the deep waters. I will never be obedient to the Man.

Narrator 1: Nobody saw him go except the little Girl Daughter. *(The little Girl Daughter sees the crab and waves at him as he enters the sea.)* The play went on until no animals were left without orders. The Eldest Magician wiped the dust off his hands and walked about the world to see how the animals were playing.

Narrator 2: He went north, Best Beloved, and found all-the-elephants-there-were digging with their tusks and stamping with their feet in the nice, new, clean earth that had been made ready for them.

Elephants: Is this right?

Eldest Magician: That is quite right. I shall breathe upon the great rocks and lumps of earth that all-the-elephants-there-were have thrown up, and turn them into the great Himalayan Mountains.

Narrator 2: He went east and found all-the-cows-there-were feeding in the fields that had been made ready for them. They licked their tongues around a whole forest at a time, then swallowed it and sat down to chew their cud.

Cows: Is that right?

Eldest Magician: It is quite right. I shall breathe upon the bare patch and turn it into the Sahara and Indian deserts.

Narrator 3: He went west and found all-the-beavers-there-were making a beaver dam across the mouths of broad rivers that had been prepared for them.

26

Beavers: Is that right?

Eldest Magician: It is quite right. I shall breathe on the fallen trees and the still water, and turn them into the Everglades in Florida.

Narrator 1: Then he went south and found all-the-turtles-there-were scratching with their flippers in the sand, which had been prepared for them. The sand and the rocks whirled through the air and fell far off into the sea.

Turtles: Is that right?

Eldest Magician: It is quite right. I shall breathe upon the sand and the rocks where they have fallen in the sea, and they will become the most beautiful islands of Borneo, Celebes, Sumatra, Java and the rest of the Malay Archipelago.

Narrator 2: The Eldest Magician met the Man on the banks of the Perak River, and said:

Eldest Magician: Ho! Son of Adam, are all the animals obedient to you?

Man: Yes.

Eldest Magician: Is all the earth obedient to you?

Man: Yes.

Eldest Magician: Is all the sea obedient to you?

Man: No. Once a day and once a night, the sea runs up the Perak River and drives the sweetwater back into the forest, so that my house is made wet. Once a day and once a night, it runs down the river and draws all the water after it, so that nothing is left but mud, and my canoe is upset. Is that the play you told it to play?'

Eldest Magician: No, that is a new and a bad play.

Man: Look. *(The Man points to the sea.)*

27

Narrator 1: As he spoke, the great sea came up the mouth of the Perak River, driving the river backwards until it flowed over all the dark forests for miles and miles, flooding the Man's house.

Eldest Magician: This is wrong. Launch your canoe and we will find out who is playing with the sea.

(The Eldest Magician, the Man and the little Girl Daughter hop into the canoe.)

Eldest Magician: Animals, which one of you is playing with the sea?

Animals: Eldest Magician, we play the plays you taught us to play—us and our children's children. Not one of us plays with the sea.

Narrator 2: The moon rose big and full over the water. On the moon was a hunchbacked old man who sat spinning a fishing line with which he hoped one day to catch the world.

Eldest Magician: Ho! Fisher of the Moon, are you playing with the sea?

Fisher of the Moon: No, I am spinning a line with which I shall someday catch the world; but I do not play with the sea.
Narrator 3: Now, there was also a Rat of the Moon that always bit the old fisherman's line as soon as he could make it.
Eldest Magician: Ho! Rat of the Moon, are you playing with the sea?'

Rat: I am too busy biting through the line that this old fisherman is spinning. I do not play with the sea.

Girl Daughter: Eldest Magician! When my father was talking to you at the Very Beginning, I saw one beast walk naughtily into the sea before you taught him his play.

Eldest Magician: How wise are little children who see and are silent! What was the beast like?

28

Girl Daughter: He was round and he was flat and his eyes grew upon stalks and he walked sideways like this. *(She crouches down and walks sideways.)* His back was covered with strong armour.

Eldest Magician: How wise are little children who speak truth! Now I know where Pau Amma went. Give me the paddle!

(He starts bashing the water with the paddle. Eventually, Pau Amma comes to the surface.)

Eldest Magician: Ah, now I know who has been playing with the sea. What are you doing, Pau Amma?

Pau Amma: Once a day and once a night, I go out to look for my food. Once a day and once a night, I return. Leave me alone.

Eldest Magician: Listen, Pau Amma. When you go out from your cave, the waters of the sea pour down into Pusat Tasek, and all the beaches of all the islands are left bare. The little fish die, and the legs of Raja Moyang Kaban, the King of the Elephants, are made muddy. When you come back and sit in Pusat Tasek, the waters of the sea rise, and half the little islands are drowned. The Man's house is flooded, and the mouth of Raja Abdullah, the King of the Crocodiles, is filled with salt water.

Pau Amma: I did not know I was so important. Now I know I will go out seven times a day, and the waters shall never be still.

Eldest Magician: I cannot make you play the play you were meant to play, Pau Amma, because you escaped me at the Very Beginning. However, if you are not afraid, come up and we will talk about it.

Pau Amma: I am not afraid. *(He rolls his eyes and folds his arms.)*

Eldest Magician: Now I will make a magic, Pau Amma, to show that you are not really important.

Narrator1: He made a magic with his left hand and, lo and behold, Best Beloved, Pau Amma's hard, blue-green-black shell fell off him just as a husk falls off a cocoa nut. Pau Amma was left as soft as the little crabs you sometimes find on the beach, Best Beloved.

29

Julie Meighan

(Pau Amma is shocked.)

Eldest Magician: Shall I ask the Man here to cut you with his knife? Shall I send for Raja Moyang Kaban, the King of the Elephants, to pierce you with his tusks, or shall I call Raja Abdullah, the King of the Crocodiles, to bite you?'

Pau Amma: I am ashamed! Give me back my hard shell and let me return to the deepest part of the ocean. I will stir out only once a day and once a night to get my food.

Eldest Magician: No, Pau Amma, I will not give you back your shell, for you will grow bigger and prouder and stronger. Perhaps you will forget your promise and play with the sea once more.
Pau Amma: What shall I do? I am so big that I can hide only in the deepest part of the ocean. If I go anywhere else all soft as I am now, the sharks and the dogfish will eat me. If I go to the deepest part of the ocean all soft as I am now, though I may be safe, I can never stir out to get my food, and so I shall die.

Eldest Magician: Pau Amma, I cannot make you play the play you were meant to play because you escaped me at the Very Beginning. However, if you choose, I can make every stone and every hole and every bunch of weeds in all the seas a safe place for you and your children for always.

Pau Amma: That is good, but I have not decided yet. Look! There is the Man who talked to you at the Very Beginning. If he had not taken your attention, I would not have grown tired of waiting and run away, and all this would never have happened. What will he do for me?'

Man: If you choose, I will make a magic so that both the deep water and the dry ground will be a home for you and your children. You will be able to hide on the land and in the sea.

Pau Amma: I have not decided yet. Look! There is the girl who saw me running away at the Very Beginning. If she had spoken then, the Eldest Magician would have called me back, and all this would never have happened. What will she do for me?'

30

Girl Daughter: If you choose, I will make a magic and give you this pair of scissors, very sharp and strong, so that when you come up from the sea to the land, you and your children can eat cocoa nuts like this all day long. Or you can use the scissors to dig a safe place for yourself that belongs to you when no stone or hole is nearby; and when the earth is too hard, by the help of these same scissors, you can run up a tree.

Pau Amma: I have not decided yet, for all soft as I am, these gifts would not help me. Give me back my shell, O Eldest Magician, and then I will play your play.

Eldest Magician: I will give it back, Pau Amma, for eleven months of the year; but on the twelfth month of every year, it shall grow soft again, to remind you and all your children that I can make magic and to keep you humble. I see that if you can run both under the water and on land, you will grow too bold; and if you can climb trees and crack nuts and dig holes with your scissors, you will grow too greedy, Pau Amma.

Pau Amma: I have decided. I will take all the gifts.

Narrator 2: Then the Eldest Magician made a magic with his right hand and, lo and behold, Best Beloved, Pau Amma grew smaller and smaller and smaller, until at last there was only a little green crab swimming in the water alongside the canoe, crying in a very small voice:

Pau Amma: Give me the scissors.

Narrator 3: The Girl Daughter picked him up and placed him in the palm of her little brown hand. She set him in the bottom of the canoe and gave him her scissors. He waved them in his little arms. He opened them and shut them and snapped them, and then said:

Pau Amma: I can eat nuts. I can crack shells. I can dig holes. I can climb trees. I can breathe in the dry air, and I can find a safe place under every stone.

Narrator 3: Pau Amma scuttled over the side of the canoe and into the water. He was so tiny that he could have hidden under the

31

shadow of a dry leaf on land or of a dead shell at the bottom of the sea.

Eldest Magician: Was that well done?

Man: Yes, but now we must return to Perak, and that is a weary way to paddle. If you hadn't made Paul Amma small, he could come out of the ocean and the water would have carried us home.

Eldest Magician: You are lazy, so your children shall be lazy. Fisher of the Moon, here is the Man too lazy to row home. Pull his canoe home with your line, fisherman.

Man: No, if I am to be lazy all my days, let the sea work for me twice a day forever. That will save me from having to paddle.

Eldest Magician: If you wish.

Narrator 1: And the Rat of the Moon stopped biting the line; and the Fisher of the Moon let down his line until it touched the sea, and he pulled the whole deep sea along, past the island of Bintang, past Singapore, past Malacca, past Selangor, until the canoe whirled into the mouth of the Perak River again.

Fisher of the Moon: Is that right?
Eldest Magician: It is quite right. See, now, that you pull the sea twice a day and twice a night forever, so that the Man may be saved from having to paddle. However, be careful not to do it too hard, or I shall make a magic on you as I did to Pau Amma.

Narrator 2: Then they all went up the Perak River and went to bed, Best Beloved.

The Beginnings of the Armadillo

Characters: Narrator; Stickly, Prickly Hedgehog; Slow and Solid Tortoise; Painted Jaguar; Monkey; Deer; Beetle; Frog; Mother Jaguar.

Narrator: Once upon a time on the banks of the Turbid Amazon, there lived a Stickly, Prickly Hedgehog.

Hedgehog: Hello, I'm the Stickly, Prickly Hedgehog. I eat shelly snails and things. *(Mimes picking up a snail and bites into it.)* Yummy! *(He rubs his tummy.)* This is my friend, the Slow and Solid Tortoise.

Tortoise: Hello, I'm the Slow and Solid Tortoise. I like to eat green leafy lettuce and things. *(He mimes picking up a head of lettuce and starts to eat it. The hedgehog and the tortoise move to stage left and are playing with each other. The Painted Jaguar enters the stage and moves to the centre.)*

Painted Jaguar: Hello, I'm the Painted Jaguar. I like to eat everything I can catch.

Monkey: Oooh, ooh, ooh, eee, eee, come and catch me, Painted Jaguar.

(Jaguar tries to catch the monkey but fails. The monkey swings from tree to tree.)

Deer: Bleat, bleat, come and catch me, Painted Jaguar.

(Jaguar tries to catch the deer but fails. The deer scampers off.)

Painted Jaguar: *(sighs)* The problem is, I'm not very good at catching anything.

Narrator: He tried to eat a frog.

Frog: Ribbit, ribbit, come and catch me, Painted Jaguar.

(Jaguar tries to catch the frog but fails. The frog hops away.)

Narrator: He tried to catch a beetle.

Beetle: Whoop, whoop, come and catch me, Painted Jaguar.

(Jaguar tries to catch the beetle but fails. The beetle scuttles off.)

Narrator: He couldn't catch any animal and he went home sad and hungry.

Mother Jaguar: You look so sad, dear. What's the matter?

Painted Jaguar: Oh, Mother, I'm so hungry. I tried to catch a monkey, a deer, a frog and a beetle and I failed … miserably.

Mother Jaguar: Listen carefully. I'll teach you how to catch a hedgehog.

Painted Jaguar: A hedgehog? But he is very prickly and stickly.

Mother Jaguar: That is true but the trick is, when you catch a hedgehog you must drop him into the water. Wait until he panics because he can't swim and then you can eat him.

Painted Jaguar: When you a catch a tortoise, you must scoop him out of his shell with your paw. Just like this. (*She mimes scooping out something with her paws.*)

Narrator: The next night, the Painted Jaguar went looking for the Sticky, Prickly Hedgehog and the Slow and Solid Tortoise. Soon he came across them.

Painted Jaguar: At last I've found you. Just in time. I'm very hungry.

Hedgehog: Oh, dear, we can't run away. He is too fast.

Tortoise: Quickly, curl up. I'll stick my head and feet into my shell.

Painted Jaguar: You two must listen to me. I have something important to say.

Hedgehog: Ignore him.

Tortoise: No problem. (*He starts to put his head in his shell.*)

Painted Jaguar: You can ignore me all you want but my mother told me that when I meet a hedgehog, I'm to drop him into water and he will uncoil. When I meet a tortoise I'm to scoop him into my paw. Now, who is who?

Hedgehog: Are you sure that's what your mother told you?

Painted Jaguar: Quite sure.

Tortoise: Quite sure? I'm sure she might have said that you uncoil the tortoise and shell him out of the water with a scoop.

Hedgehog: And when you paw a hedgehog, you must drop him into your paw.

Tortoise: Maybe she said that when you water a hedgehog you must shell him until he

Painted Jaguar: Oh dear, I'm confused now. I don't know what my mother said.

Hedgehog: Let's explain it more clearly. When you scoop water, you uncoil it.

Tortoise: When you pour meat, you drop it into a tortoise with a scoop.

34

Hedgehog: Is it clear now?

Painted Jaguar: No, my brain hurts. Just tell me which one of you is the hedgehog and which is the tortoise.

Hedgehog: I couldn't possibly tell you that but you can scoop me out if you wish.

Painted Jaguar: Then you must be the tortoise.

Narrator: The Painted Jaguar stuck out his paw to scoop out the hedgehog, but just then the hedgehog curled up. The Painted Jaguar's paw was filled with pricks.

Painted Jaguar: Ouch, you are not the tortoise. You are Stickly, Prickly Hedgehog.

Tortoise: I'm the tortoise. If you want to uncoil me, drop me into the water.

Painted Jaguar: You've mixed everything up. I'm so confused. I don't know if I'm on my painted head or painted tail. My mother told me to drop one of you into the water.

(He throws the tortoise into the water. The Painted Jaguar as the Slow and Solid Tortoise swims away.)

Tortoise: You can't catch me now, tortoise.

Hedgehog: Ha, ha, bye-bye, Painted Jaguar.

(The Painted Jaguar returns home weary and dejected.)

Mother Jaguar: What's the matter, son? What have you done to your poor painted paw?

Painted Jaguar: I tried to scoop something that said he wanted to be scooped out of his shell.

Mother Jaguar: Your paw is full of prickles. You must have tried to scoop the hedgehog. You should have dropped the hedgehog into the water.

Painted Jaguar: I did that to the other animal. I haven't eaten all day and I'm sooooo hungry.

Mother Jaguar: Listen carefully. A hedgehog curls in so his prickles stick out and he can't swim.

(Hedgehog and tortoise are hiding in the bushes, listening carefully.) A tortoise cannot curl up but he can draw his head and legs into his shell. He is a good swimmer.

Painted Jaguar: That's easy. I've got it.

Can't curl but can swim, Slow and Solid Tortoise, that's him.

Curls up but can't swim, Stickly, Prickly Hedgehog, that's him.

Tortoise: He'll never forget that.

Hedgehog: We need to do something.

Tortoise: I'll teach you how to swim

Hedgehog: And I'll teach you how to curl up. That will fool the Painted Jaguar.

Narrator: They practiced by the banks of the Turbid Amazon. *(The tortoise practises curling and the hedgehog practises swimming.)*

Tortoise: We've done it. I can curl and you can swim.

Hedgehog: You look different.

Tortoise: So, do you.

Narrator: They saw the Painted Jaguar walking along the banks of the river. He was still nursing his sore paw.

Hedgehog: Morning, Painted Jaguar.

Painted Jaguar: Good morning. I know who you are. You are the hedgehog. You can't swim.

Hedgehog: Oh yes, I can. Look.

(Hedgehog jumps in the river and starts swimming.)

Painted Jaguar: You are the tortoise. You can't curl.

Tortoise: Oh yes, I can. Look.

(Tortoise curls up. The Painted Jaguar looks confused and runs off.)

Tortoise & Hedgehog: That got rid of him, ha, ha.

Painted Jaguar: Mother, Mother, there were two animals by the Turbid Amazon. The one you said can't curl, can and the other one who can't swim, can. I'm so confused.

Mother Jaguar: A hedgehog is a hedgehog. A tortoise is a tortoise. They can never be anything else.

Painted Jaguar: They are a bit of both and I don't know their proper names.

Mother Jaguar: Everything should have a name. Let's call them armadillos and you shouldn't touch them.

Narrator: Painted Jaguar did as he was told. Ever since that day, every hedgehog and every tortoise on the Turbid Amazon has been called an armadillo.

I've never sailed the Amazon,
I've never reached Brazil;
But the *Don* and *Magdalena*,
They can go there when they will!

Yes, weekly from Southampton,
Great steamers, white and gold,
Go rolling down to Rio
 (Roll down roll down to Rio!)
And I'd like to roll to Rio
Some day before I'm old!

I've never seen a Jaguar,
Nor yet an Armadill—
O dilloing in his armour,
And I s'pose I never will,
Unless I go to Rio
These wonders to behold
Roll down roll down to Rio
Roll really down to Rio!
Oh, I'd love to roll to Rio

Julie Meighan

The Butterfly Who Stamped

Characters: Three Narrators, King, Balkis, Butterfly, Butterfly's Wife, Gull Winged Djinn, Six Wives/Queens.

Narrator 1: This is the story of The Butterfly Who Stamped and it happened just so.

Narrator 2: Long, long ago when the world was nearly new and all.

Narrator 3: There was a lovely garden full of orange trees and roses.

Narrator 1: In the middle of the garden was a great, golden palace.

Narrator 2: In the middle of that great golden palace were 999 queens. *(The queens walk on the stage one by one. Queen 1 is carrying a tray with a pot of tea and several cups. Queen 2 is carrying a plate with a large cake.)*

Narrator 3: In the middle of the 999 queens was the wise and benevolent King Sulmain-bin-Daoud. Some of the wives were nice but some were horrid.

Queen 1: I've made you a nice pot of tea for all the wives.

Queen 2: I've been baking all day. Who would like some cake?

Queen 3: No thanks, your cakes don't taste very good.

Queen 4: And your tea is always so weak.

Queen 5: Why do you have to be so horrid all the time?

Queen 6: Why do you have to be so nice?

King: *(Walks onstage, looks on in despair.)* What am I going to do? My wives are so quarrelsome all the time. I'm so powerful, I can turn this ring on my finger and summon the great Gull Winged Djinn. He'll know what to do. *(He twists his ring and the Gull Winged Djinn appears.)*

Gull Winged Djinn: What is your command, master?

King: I don't know what to do with my 999 quarrelsome queens.

Gull Winged Djinn: I could magic all your 999 quarrelsome queens into white mules of the desert. Or camels. Or even pomegranate seeds.

Narrator 1: The king was too kind to magic his wives into white mules of the desert.

38

Narrator 2: Or camels.

Narrator 3: Or pomegranate seeds.

(The wives are quarrelling in the background.)

King: I can't stand this quarrelling anymore. I'm going for a walk in my beautiful garden to find my first and most loved queen, Balkis. She is the most beautiful and wise of all my 999 queens.

(He walks out into the garden. He sees Balkis and hugs her.)

Balkis: Hello, love of my life, light of my eyes, Can I ask you a favour?

King: Of course, I'll do anything for you.

Balkis: Please turn the ring on your finger.

King: Why?

Balkis: I want you to show all those quarrelsome queens how powerful you are and teach them a lesson.

King: I would love to grant your wish but I fear if I did that, I would be boasting.

Balkis: Well, you're going to have to come up with a plan to stop the quarrels.

King: I know. If I sit underneath my favourite camphor tree and meditate, I might come up with some answers.

Balkis: I'll leave you to come up with a plan. *(She whispers to the audience.)* I'll hide behind that bush *(points to a bush onstage)* so I can secretly watch over him.

Narrator 1: The king fell asleep under the tree but he woke up to the sound of quarrelling.

King: Those quarrelsome queens have followed me to the garden. What am I to do? *(He looks around.)* Hold on, it's not the queens but these two little butterflies.

Butterfly's Wife: You're so lazy. You never help around the flower. I must do all the work.

Butterfly: Really, wife, I don't know why you keep insulting me. Don't you know I only have to stamp my foot and this great golden palace and lovely garden would immediately vanish in a clap of thunder?

King: Ha, ha, that's funny. It has made me forget about my quarrelsome queens. Little butterfly, come here.

Butterfly's Wife: All your lies are catching up with you. The king has overheard you.

Butterfly: The king has summoned me. I'm frightened but I better show my wife how brave I am or else I'll never hear the end of it.

King: Little butterfly, why did you tell that massive lie to your wife?

Butterfly: Please forgive me, your majesty *(he bows)*, but she is always arguing with me. I can't get her to stop. You must know what wives are like. You do have 999 quarrelsome queens living in your palace.

King: Ha, ha. I do know what wives are like. Now, return to your wife so I can hear what you say to her. *(Butterfly goes back to his wife and the king sneaks up behind them to listen to their conversation.)*

Butterfly's Wife: The king heard you. He must have been very angry with you. Serves you right for telling all those fibs.

Butterfly: I don't care who hears me. I'm not frightened of anyone. He very kindly asked me not to stamp, as he would like to keep his golden palace and beautiful garden safe. They cost a lot of money. Out of kindness, I agreed I wouldn't stamp.

Butterfly Wife: Goodness gracious me.

King: Ha, ha. *(The butterflies are unaware that the king is listening and the king is unaware that Balkis sees everything from behind the bush.)*

Balkis: While my husband selflessly cares for these two creatures, I think I can find a way to save him from the 999 quarrelsome queens. Butterfly's Wife, come here please

Butterfly's Wife: Yes, your majesty.

Balkis: Do you believe your husband?

Butterfly's Wife: Of course not. I just pretend to be impressed to keep him happy. You must know what husbands are like.

Balkis: Well I have a plan. The next time he threatens to stamp, tell him to go ahead. That will put an end to his boasting.

Narrator 1: The butterflies flew away but the next day they were quarrelling worse than ever.

Butterfly: Wife, you should remember what I can do if I stamp my foot.

Butterfly's Wife: Go ahead, I dare you to do it. Go ahead and stamp.

Butterfly: Be careful what you ask for, wife.

(Butterfly flies off to the king.)

Butterfly: My wife wants me to stamp. What am I to do? Help, please. She'll never stop laughing if I don't stamp and make the palace and gardens disappear.

King: No, she won't. When I'm finished, she'll never laugh at you again.

Narrator 1: The king turned his magic ring on his finger. The great Gull Winged Djinn appeared.

Gull Winged Djinn: You called, your majesty? *(He bows.)*

King: When this butterfly stamps his feet, you will make my palace and gardens disappear in a clap of thunder. When he stamps again, they will return.

Gull Winged Djinn: Your wish is my command.

King: Butterfly, go back to your wife. *(Butterfly returns to his wife.)*

Butterfly's Wife: Oh, there you are. Go ahead and stamp your foot.

Butterfly: I will. *(He stamps his foot.)*

Narrator 2: The Gull Winged Djinn jerked the palace and the garden a thousand miles into the air.

Narrator 1: Everything turned black. There was a loud thunder clap.

Butterfly's Wife: Goodness gracious, I'll never doubt you again. Put everything back. We need that beautiful garden to live in. *(Butterfly stamps again.)*

Narrator 2: Very carefully, the Gull Winged Djinn returned the palace and the garden.

(The lights come back on.)

(The queens run onstage.)

Queen 1: What happened?

Queen 2: That was so scary.

Queen 3: One minute we were busy quarrelling in the palace.

Queen 4: And the next minute there was a loud thunder clap.

Queen 5: And then we were in darkness.

Queen 6: I've never been so happy to see the other wives.

Balkis: Calm down and I'll explain what happened. A butterfly complained to the king about his wife and the king decided to teach her a lesson.

Queen 1: Oh dear, if the king did this because a quarrelsome butterfly.

Queen 2: What will he do to us, as we have annoyed him so much?

Queen 3: We have been quarrelling for years.

Queen 4: Maybe we should try to get on with one another.

Queen 5: Let's go back to the palace and have a nice cup of tea.

Queen 6: And a nice piece of cake.

King: The queens have stopped quarrelling. When did this marvellous thing happen?

Balkis: That's my little secret.

Narrator 2: Everyone lived together happily and peacefully. Forever and ever.

Narrator 1: As did the butterfly's wife and the boastful butterfly himself.

Butterfly: I'm the first and last butterfly ever in the world to stamp.

There was never a Queen like Balkis,
From here to the wide world's end;
But Balkis talked to a butterfly
As you would talk to a friend.

There was never a King like Solomon,
Not since the world began;
But Solomon talked to a butterfly
As a man would talk to a man.

She was Queen of Sabha
And *he* was Asia's Lord
But they both of 'em talked to butterflies
When they took their walks abroad.

The Sing Song of Old Man Kangaroo

Characters: Two narrators, Kangaroo, Dingo, Nga, Ngong, Nguing.

Narrator 1: This is the story of the Sing Song of Old Man Kangaroo and it happened just so.

Narrator 2: Long, long ago when the world was new and all, there lived a kangaroo who was very different than he is now.

Narrator 1: The kangaroo liked to dance on a rock in the middle of Australia.

(Kangaroo enters the stage, he is dancing and enjoying himself.)

Kangaroo: Hello everyone! I'm the Kangaroo. I dance every day on this rock, but no one ever takes any notice of me. I think it is because I'm too grey and woolly and my four legs are far too short. I fancy a change.

Narrator 2: The kangaroo decided to ask the little god Nga to help him, at six before breakfast.

Nga: *(yawns and stretches)* What do you want? It's very early.

Kangaroo: Make me different from all the other animals by five this afternoon.

Nga: I'm far too busy sleeping to listen to this nonsense. Go away.

Narrator 1: He decided to ask the middle god Nguing to help him, at eight after breakfast.

Kangaroo: Make me different from all other animals; make me, also, wonderfully popular by five this afternoon.

Nguing: I'm far too busy working to listen to this nonsense. Go away.

Narrator 1: The Kangaroo decided to ask the big god Ngong to help him at ten before dinner.

Kangaroo: Make me different from all other animals; make me popular and a wonderful runner by five this afternoon.

Narrator 2: Up jumped Nqong from his bath in the salt pan and shouted.

Ngong: Of course, I will help you. Dingo! Wake up, Dingo! Do you see that gentleman dancing on the rock over there? He wants to be popular and very truly run after. Dingo, make him SO!

Dingo: *(jumps up)* What, that cat-rabbit?' *(Dingo points at the kangaroo who is dancing.)*

Narrator 1: Off ran Dingo, hungry and grinning like a coal-scuttle, after Kangaroo.

Kangaroo: Why does that vicious dingo look like he wants to eat me?

Dingo: That's because I do want to eat you. I'm very hungry.

Narrator 1: The kangaroo ran as fast as he could with his little bunny legs.

Narrator 2: He ran through the mountains;

Narrator 1: he ran through the salt-pans;

Narrator 2: he ran through the reed beds;

Narrator 1: he ran through the blue gums;

Narrator 2: he ran through the spinifex.

Kangaroo: I'm exhausted and my little front legs ache.

Dingo: I'm still behind you, Kangaroo. I'm getting hungrier and hungrier.

Kangaroo: He is still behind me, grinning like a rat trap, never getting nearer, never getting farther.

Narrator 1: He ran through the ti-trees;

Narrator 2: he ran through the mulga;

Narrator 1: he ran through the long grass;

Narrator 2: he ran through the short grass;

Narrator 1: he ran through the Tropics of Capricorn and Cancer.

Kangaroo: I'm exhausted and my little hind legs ache.

Dingo: I'm still behind you, Kangaroo. I'm getting hungrier and hungrier.

Kangaroo: He is still behind me, grinning like a rat trap, never getting nearer, never getting farther.

Narrator 1: The kangaroo came to the Wollongong River.

Narrator 2: Now, there wasn't any bridge,

Narrator 1: and there wasn't any ferry boat,

Narrator 2: So, the Kangaroo had to think on his feet.

Kangaroo: I'll just have to take a chance and hop over the Wollongong River.

Narrator 1: He hopped through the Flinders;

Narrator 2: he hopped through the Cinders;

Narrator 1: he hopped through the deserts in the middle of Australia.

Narrator 2: First, he hopped one yard;

Narrator 1: then he hopped three yards;

Narrator 2: then he hopped five yards.

Kangaroo: My legs have grown stronger and longer from all this hopping.

Dingo: I'm bemused by all this hopping. Whoever heard of a hopping Kangaroo? How will I get him to stop?

Narrator 1: Then up from the salt-pans came the big god Ngong.

Ngong: Stop. It's five o clock.

Kangaroo: Thank goodness that's over.

Ngong: Why aren't you grateful to Yellow-Dog Dingo? Why don't you thank him for all he has done for you?'

Kangaroo: He's chased me out of the home of my childhood; he's chased me out of my regular mealtime; he's altered my shape, so I'll never get it back; and he's played Old Scratch with my legs.

Ngong: Perhaps I'm mistaken, but didn't you ask me to make you different from all other animals, as well as to make you very truly sought after? And now it is five o'clock.

Kangaroo: I wish that I hadn't. I thought you would do it by charms and incantations, but this seems like a practical joke.

Ngong: A joke, say that again and I'll whistle up Dingo and he will run your hind legs off.

Kangaroo: I must apologize. Legs are legs, and you needn't alter 'em so far as I am concerned. I only meant to explain to Your Lordliness that I've had nothing to eat since morning, and I'm very empty indeed.

Dingo: I am just in the same situation. I've made him different from all other animals, but what may I have for my tea?

Ngong: Come and ask me about it tomorrow, because I'm going to wash.

Narrator 1: So, they were left in the middle of Australia, Old Man Kangaroo and Yellow-Dog Dingo, and each said…

Kangaroo and Dingo: This is all your fault.

This is the mouth-filling song
Of the race that was run by a Boomer,
Run in a single burst — only event of its kind —
Started by Big GHod Nqong from Warrigaborrigarooma,
Old Man Kangaroo first : Yellow-Dog Dingo behind.

Kangaroo bounded away,
His back-legs working like pistons —
Bounded from morning till dark,
Twenty-five feet to a bound.

Yellow-Dog Dingo lay
Like a yellow cloud in the distance -
Much too busy to bark.
My! but they covered the ground !

Nobody knows where they went,
Or followed the track that they flew in,
For that Continent
Hadn't been given a name.
They ran thirty degrees,
From Torres Straits to the Leeuwin
(Look at the Atlas, please),
And they ran back as they came.

S'posing you could trot
From Adelaide to the Pacific,
For an afternoon's run -
Half what these gentlemen did —
You would feel rather hot,
But your legs would develop terrific —
Yes, my importunate son,
You'd be a Marvellous Kid !

Other Books by the Author:

Drama Start Series:

Drama Start: Drama Activities, Plays and Monologues for Children (Ages 3-8)

Drama Start Two: Drama Activities for Children (Ages 9-12)

Stage Start: 20 Plays for Children (Ages 3-12)

Stage Start: Two: 20 More Plays for Children (Ages 3-12)

Movement Start: Over 100 Movement Activities and Stories for Children

ESL Drama Start: Drama Activities and Plays for ESL Learners

On Stage Series:

Fairy Tales on Stage: A Collection of Plays for Children

Classics on Stage: A Collection of Plays Based on Classic Children's Stories

Aesop's Fables on Stage: A Collection of Plays Based on Aesop's Fables

Christmas Stories on Stage: A Collection of Plays for Children

Panchatantra on Stage: A Collection of Plays for Children

Hans Christian Andersen's Stories on Stage: A Collection of Plays for Children

Oscar Wilde's Stories on Stage: A Collection of Plays based on Oscar Wilde's Short Stories